THE HOUSE YOU WERE BORN IN

THE HUGH MACLENNAN POETRY SERIES

Editors: Allan Hepburn and Carolyn Smart

Recent titles in the series

The House You Were Born In

TANYA STANDISH MCINTYRE

McGill-Queen's University Press

Montreal & Kingston • London • Chicago

ISBN 978-0-2280-1464-5 (paper)
ISBN 978-0-2280-1578-9 (ePDF)
ISBN 978-0-2280-1579-6 (ePUB)

Legal deposit fourth quarter 2022
Bibliothèque nationale du Québec

Printed in Canada on acid-free paper that is 100% ancient forest free
(100% post-consumer recycled), processed chlorine free

Funded by the Government of Canada — Financé par le gouvernement du Canada

Canadä

Conseil des arts du Canada — Canada Council for the Arts

We acknowledge the support of the Canada Council for the Arts.

Nous remercions le Conseil des arts du Canada de son soutien.

Library and Archives Canada Cataloguing in Publication

Title: The house you were born in / Tanya Standish McIntyre.

Names: McIntyre, Tanya, author.

Series: Hugh MacLennan poetry series.

Description: Series statement: The Hugh MacLennan
   poetry series | Poems.

Identifiers: Canadiana (print) 20220408416 | Canadiana (ebook)
   20220408432 | ISBN 9780228014645 (softcover) |
   ISBN 9780228015789 (ePDF) | ISBN 9780228015796 (ePUB)

Classification: LCC PS8625.I595 H68 2022 | DDC C811/.6—dc23

This book was typeset by Marquis Interscript in 9.5/13 Sabon.

For my grandfather,
Lloyd George Standish (1928–1996),
and for my mother

CONTENTS

Contents

THE HOUSE YOU WERE BORN IN

*Tell me how much you know of the sufferings
of your fellow men and I will tell you how much
you have loved them.*

Helmut Thielicke

Our mother tongue did not have a word
for how the river wore away the stone
without meaning to;

for the shadows made when August
fell through the leaves; for the dirt – the taste
of it, that home was built on;

for the one small handful of words
that make a stranger not a stranger;

for the shattered emerald
body of the ebony jewelwing,
born only a fortnight past; for
           the memory of a memory;

for how we long to come to a full stop
that is not
           death.

What lived
in the walls left
arms to hang in
resignation, hemmed
by the rustling
calico.

The sill was
scattered with the wire
legs of flies but in May
by the door were new-born
shoots of sumac – I skinned
their velvet stems, leaving
only the skeleton.

In the distance was a figure no
one could name; two black willows
remained after the hurricane – one
arched back in its declension: a hand
receiving its pasture.

Under a simmering
parasol, a threshold of trees; wedded
wood; a pall of leaves: witness
bearers – even our road
was like that.

If you look behind the barn, maybe
you still can see
the old sentry, wind's cully –
the white pine in a low bow to the town.

If it is early June, there will be wild
strawberries – in an old book
I read it is bad luck
to eat anything picked in a graveyard.

Stones for the babies are flat
to the ground, grown into the sod,
etched with the names no one hears
anymore: Sadie, Percy, Tymandra.

As their mothers
once did, I pull grass from the edges,
making green frames pretty
against the red
strawberries.

They are stuck
behind the peeling sound
of rotting cellophane – two pictures of
the handsome couple signing
their names, heavy
pens in their hands – she is
nineteen in an apricot
eyelet dress; his hair longer
than I remember, his eleven more
years captured in the shot, and
you want to reach in, knock those weighted
pens from their hands, light a fire
under the card table draped
with the lace cloth, any minor
distraction that allows them
to flee, to run
and never look back, but
it cannot be
altered – a course has been set,
profiles locked in a cameo
the colour of the dress, dreams turned
to face the back of the frame, wall-
papered over, erased
with flour-paste – they must sign
a vow that she will not
study art; that he will not
start his own garage – damn
the pen that flows with ease, the ink
being my blood – I bind them, saying yes
to being born, with no apologies.

An only child, she does not leave
her home; he will be added on, a weak
weld at best, a town-kid
on a farm where mixing
blood comes with a price, an X
marking the spot at the edge
of the field
where the house trailer will sit.

The calendar on the wall
by the phone
will change many times
while the heart sputters to start
like a flooded engine – the clock
is patient; it will take a long time
before the rod is finally
thrown, piercing through
the block – there is
no happy

ending and how it was all there to see,
in the stiff bend of their arms, the angle
they held the pen – they did not see it
frame by frame, the endless
unraveling, but they saw the brick
wall the car was bound for; they heard
the sound of cellophane, the peeling
of tires but still hoped
the held-down horn outside
the hall festooned with garland
might be for someone else.

ONE BODY

I am almost five
by the blue bathroom basin, yanking up
my Orlon romper – then the feeling
that comes without warning, of something too
big, that would swallow me whole, but smaller
than a needle's eye –

How can it be
when it was next to impossible, that here
was where I was put? Here, placed in this particular
body and not somewhere, anywhere else?

In an order that made bathtubs and doorstops
    and toasters,
impossible things of every shape, size, and colour, things
we call things, and more of these things, that all began
with What?

Then, the dreaded inching-up of panic, not
unlike coming up and out of
my own skin – I bang through the green
screen door to the old white dog under
the mountain-ash

that grows too close, they say,
to the corner
of the house – oh, let them not
cut it, please God *(one of many prayers)*:
I am almost tall enough to fit
my hand into the cleft and then
I can climb to the top – how

strange the way we learn to live
in one body, for as long as something
gauges it should last – how strange
how we become

heavy, so heavy
that no one can catch us
when we fall, from even the nearest
handhold, from even
the lowest branch.

At the Formica table, they drink tea
with canned milk, while I sit on the floor
in the ramparts
of furniture legs, looking for something
I have not yet seen in that odd collection

of books: bound in a grainy orange,
Indian Herbal embossed in black, with the profile
of a chief in feathered headdress – tiny print in columns;
   sea to sea
testimonials: "At long last cured of palsy, dropsy, and boils"
by the mail-order miracle of horsetail and cleavers,
   slippery elm
and such – next,

the *Encyclopedia of Animals*, beginning
with the (lesser) pygmy shrew – something has spilled
in the serpents, sticking the pages shut, affixing
the adder to the pea-hen, the boa to the pea-cock
(I did not but wish I had known then the tale
of how in a transmutation of sorts,
the glory of the peacock's plumage owes
to its noxious snake-eating habits) – then

are Anderson's stories, which I handle with the carefullest
of care, so as not to let it open to the cherry-haired
match girl, in the seconds just before,
with her last flame – she has a look
in her eyes
that I cannot abide, in a heartless
watercolour blizzard.

BLACK RASPBERRIES

A border of black raspberry
bushes were left when they cleared the new
yard where my feet beat bare a path
in the hard earth held by maple
roots, past mother with her basket
of wet clothes to hang on the line
between two trees that, to me,
are brothers.

I cook both ripe and unripe
berries in my play house, in a blue
plastic pan, add real salt and pepper
to serve to my grandfather on plantain leaves
with a sprig of moss – he is so deft
at pretending to eat them, the game becomes more
his than mine – I learn to pretend better
than anyone, anything to make him
laugh, always: anything.

Each day I inspect
the bushes behind my little house
for newness, tiny thorns
holding fast to my arms as I stretch toward
the blackest deep within
or I take to my horse
on springs that I keep
behind my house, so no one sees
how wild we gallop,
the up and down
shriek of the springs
nearly breaking, the hollow
metal frame for moments
lifting off the ground.

LES FRUITS

Fruit being mandatory for "snack"
in kindergarten, bashed-in Macintosh
apples knock around
in lunch boxes some call "pails,"
though they are not
pails, definitely boxes, airtight plastic
boxes ideal for fermenting fruit – mine is blue
to match my raincoat, with Snoopy the dog
on the cover, which makes me sad and why
is hard to say.

Overripe bananas, pears
turned to pulp (they must have
seemed fine the night before; no mother
could be so cruel) but above all else, it is
our oldest sense, cells reaching back
to the limbic brain, that will
forever connote days spent under the watch
of knickered Tante Danielle – like the Kuiper belt,
the smell orbits our circle of seven
five-year-olds with legs folded
"Indian-style" for snack.

The tapping sound of a pointer
on a laminated paper, over and over
la banane, la poire, la pomme.
One day, Roger has a plum, exotic
fare, and will not be convinced it is
la prune – I sympathize deeply, equally
unsold on *le raisin*
being a grape.

On the bus ride home that takes an hour
to get fifteen minutes, the yellow Blue
Bird bus crisscrossing back roads, I plan
what I will tell the ones who ask
"and what did you do *today?*"

French words for fruit, the daily
minor injustices that seem anything but
minor, the pointer and
the pointlessness, the problem
with my lunch box, fruitless
are my efforts to explain.

They must be right and we must be
wrong – at school I learn there are things
I must never say:

I must not call scissors *shears*, must not
add *miller* after moth, I must not call
a splinter a *sliver*, an iron for clothes
a *flat-iron* – I must say a *bit* and not a *speck*,
I must not ask a kid how they *made out*
on a test, nor call a driveway
a *dooryard*, an outlet a *plug-in*, a robe
a *housecoat*, or a couch a *chesterfield* – I can
yank on a book stuck in my bookbag, but
I cannot *reef*.

When my name is called, I must
answer not with *what*, but *yes*, or risk
being sentenced
to walk the schoolyard plank
with the recess monitor,
a school-mate of my mother who calls her
Winnie, mother of Timmy
with the warts and snotty nose,
while the rest
gather in clusters like happy
grapes, playing make-believe
games by the tree, taking turns
finding reasons to laugh
at a kid who uses words
like me.

How to galvanize tin
      vulcanize rubber
carburize steel
      true north versus magnetic
AC versus DC
          radar
          humpback whales
          Disraeli, Churchill, Himmler, Hitler
          Lake Titicaca, Aboriginals, Pygmies
mummies, piranhas

Detroit locker
power-take-off
a two versus four-stroke engine
diesel versus gas

A fisher, a weasel, a mink
          lynx compared to a bobcat
          grizzly versus black

How to sharpen the sickle
                    on a mowing machine
            cut glass under water with shears
How to tell the woodgrain of maple
                    oak
            walnut
        ash
What a governor does on a tractor
                    the names of plants and trees
How to build a house: Saw
                    a log lengthwise
(a trench, two men, and a saw)

Stars and planets orbiting the sun
                            asteroids and meteors
                            diamonds and coal mines
                            fossils lodged in amber
How to gauge where
a cut tree
                will fall
which in part cannot be conveyed

                        the year Cockshutt merged
                            with Oliver
                        when Ferguson took Harris
a 30.06 versus 308
versus a 303
                        Remington compared to Winchester
                        bolt-action versus lever

Sherman tanks, the South Pacific, nuclear submarines
William Lyon Mackenzie King, Louis St Laurent

The *Titanic*'s velvet,
      her boiler rooms, the ballroom chandelier
            the *Lusitania* sinking
                the sound
    of words we love and hate, for reasons only
      we understand –

my grandfather and I talk
      about things like this
           and worlds and worlds more
while the rest
      go for silly Sunday drives
and think I must be bored.

SUGARING

Hundred year old maples joined in a ring
around our house, roots grown through the wall
of our cellar; cellar of the deep stone well, the yawling
prisoner cat; cellar of revenants, wraiths
and chains – stories they would tell at night to cure
anyone of sleep. In March, up from the earth, by
some magical ancient osmosis, with the faint taste of
bananas, sap rose with steady drips, overflowing
our galvanized buckets from a hole bored in
the pulpy layers with a red-handled bit stock.

How sealed within
a case we are, as children, before words
let us out; how dusk deepens, pressing into
the belly, as though day
would take us with it – all day I shattered
layers of pond ice with a stick, releasing
more and more to the stream, the glass music lost
and found, until I could not feel my hands.

Wood smoke wound with our syrup
made its way west to the hills – a winter's end
offering to forgotten gods, who watched us
but never intervened – gods whom
by then, had abandoned all
of them, but me.

Down, the road forked in a Y,
just past Leo's barn, on the way
to one town or the other; up,
it passed the maples, the horse
chestnut we planted, all the way
to the top of the field
where the wind blew
perpetual warning, over the hill
where the black cat
would end his days, on our way
up to the woods along the old potato
field, rolling over the wild-
flowers that would spring back up
behind us; old Mutt on airborne
paws, longing for a rabbit, pink
flapping tongue, black happy eyes, me
on the running board holding tight
to the wheel's red well;
driving back, we give way to wind
like a door swung wide
open; down
the road and higher notes
of changing gears, turning in
down below
the hedge, then
back up
around
into the dooryard.

The black on white of winter
layers, summer gradients of green;
horizons of fences, stone walls, back roads, endless
lines of trees; the skyline etching into
forever as the hills rise north to
mountains, the lake; the far-off lights
of town from the bathroom
window where I wished
upon a star that you would live
when you were sick, down
to the swale-grass in the far wet corner
the mowing machine will miss

the white birches standing in the ice-
bucket spring, where butter
once was kept, then south all
the way to the culvert, a day's walk, say
you stopped to look
at things, like the soft brown nose

of a weasel
poking from a sandy hole; gather
green butternuts, sticky as antler
velvet, or have a picnic on the giant
rock of pickled eggs, saltines, and a jar
of tea; admire a hops vine's ruffled cones;
hunt blackberries hot in the mouth
from sun, or study the tracks of
animals who wended their way
unseen, hidden from all
the world, in the old tunnel
of ironwood,
cherry, ash, beech,
basswood and balm of Gilead.

From the road, from the house
it was a green glass orb
in summer, the copse
of maple and ash just before the field
sloped down; only once within
did you see

it was a world
unto itself, self-contained – it was
a place that would acknowledge
you, would say: "Ah, it is you, and just
yesterday your mother
and Wendy were playing
right here," gesturing to
the rusted tin cups,
saucers strewn amidst
the bloodroot; it was a testament
to things unchanged, a dollhouse
forest where a pair of woodchucks
raised their yearly young – from the house
you could see them basking
on their haunches, when the sky
turned like a kaleidoscope
every shade of coral and
crimson, before dusk
in its thickness, released memory
like pollen, from events
bound in root-knots miles
underground – you could hear it

in the breeze sweeping the tops
of the trees, a sound of layered skirts
skimming a plank floor – as though
all things
were conscious

of their place
at dusk, simply bearing
the given, and each participating
thing took hold anew, pulling the knot
in tighter to a solemnity that hushed
one and all, save
the bullfrog, its giant
mouth choking a bellow
so hoarse and deep,
it cued a starlit dirge
at a perennial vigil:

the frogs
in their silken black mud knew
there was always
a soul for whom to mourn.

The Jock
house, the Ashman
woods, Cramer's bridge, Ruth
Brown's; a long
front veranda, taken over
with vine, peeling
papered walls of what once was
a kitchen, the season blowing in
where a door
had hung – the place
having fallen, a picture
was held
by a name, the title
of a story
worth the telling: homage
to ones who not only had
died, but lived,
becoming a thought
in the form of a word
that held their passage, a loving
kind of
affection, as though a light
shone from behind
the word itself,
from a lamp once
lit and not yet
extinguished.

Not a thing was
kempt as it had been,
once, though
the oldest folks could still recall
the wagons and carts that came
from miles around, such was
the beauty of the rare
climbing roses, paths
mown through fields upon which
to promenade, the apricot bells
of the foxglove; the scent of the lilac hedges,
milk-white lattice arbors and somewhere
stuck in the leaves
of an encyclopaedia of once
general-knowledge, lost
on a shelf no one can reach, a silver-plate
photograph
in perfect dark and light reveals
the lace-gloved ladies, parasols of filmy
netting; gentlemen in tailcoats and top hats,
the sun-lit ribboned ringlets
of little boys dressed in frocks
picnicking in the dappled
shade of our maple copse.

Mother would sit, thinking
she called it, out of eyesight
from the rest, down by the culvert
below the bank of the road
that divided pasture from field – she was caught
in the plot, conflicts of characters
in a play more real than life
because it was
our life. It came all the way
from the cedar swamp, the spring-fed
stream, the best for miles around,
ice-cold and clear along the lane
where cows trod paths
coming home under evening apples.

In her silence I strip bark
from twigs, masts for leaf-boats
set sail on the stream,
though they upend and are whisked away
wrong-side-up, upside-down, drowning
all passengers, bodies never
recovered, remembered only by trinities
of blood-
red trilliums – stinking-johns,
we call them, and we know
they are rare.

I want a boat
to make it to Leo's
pond, said to be
dangerously deep, invisible
to us, though we know
it is there, behind his round
red barn. We hear the splash
of his boys diving in: Unlike us,
the French have no fear
of drowning.

I try and try
to whistle a blade
of witch-grass between my thumbs;
I want to
make a three-note flute
but have no knife with which to
whittle; we stay
forever
under the old black elm, the last
of its kind, slowly dying.

We drove to a park of trees
up on the highway, once
mother had her license, a park
in later years you would never know
had existed – we sat on swings when things
shook in a way imperceptible
to humans, like a dam
risen a drop or two beyond
its purpose – she would talk, I would listen
like a younger sister, accepting, taking in
the studied womanly art never meant to be
perfected, of reconciling resignation
with acceptance, linking back
to the distant past, looping around
to present, as if
discerning a pattern alone
could veer even a tendril
off onto a direction of its own – the elm
in that park was bound
with a vine that grew into its bark
like old wire
along the trunk, forked
from its inception, beginning
beneath the ground, fused
with the root, as if
born of the same
innocence.

One
morning each summer
early, before the sky took
colour, we would load up
things and by this
side of ten we
would be at Bear
River.

With stiff knees we
would walk to the banks
of that still near-
thick brown river,
with dark wonder
stare down into
the deep a marvel
of horror.

The rest of the way
to the sea I would think
of that still near-
thick brown river,
the slow and hideous
death I would meet
sinking slow down
to the bottom.

When at last
the road ended we
would stop to revere
the sea we never
expected the edge
of the world met the sky
and the wind, the air
crisp and foreign.

That night
we would sleep
in the damp
inn sheets to the sound
of never and always
wake to the scream
of gulls and then stuff
our clothes back in
Samsonite cases,

faring well to
the salt the swell
the swirl the sweep
of the dizzying sand,
to the roaring
beast that swallowed each
drop of the brown
Bear River.

THE BUICK

In the garage
where we cracked the velvet cases
of butternuts in the vice, kept
in its own dark room, long and golden nut-
brown was the Buick,
brought out only a handful of times
in summer, driven slow and smooth
to the White Mountains, where the sun glinted off
its metallic flake at every roadside
attraction that caught my eye, paths
that led to waterfalls, words on wooden
signposts: "In this place, in the year of … a man
named … came upon a curious thing"; remarkable
rocks, precarious lookouts – only twice,
did it feel rain – its tawny patterned seats encased
in a flat kind of bubble-wrap held fast
the smell of newness, Old Spice aftershave, Black
Diamond pipe tobacco sticking out
from the pocket of my grandfather's
short-sleeved, red-checked shirt;
his long elbow out the window, slow-
coasting down the hot
highway river, our smiling
cow bobbing
from the rearview mirror,
the tiny bell around her neck softly
ringing as we lick the salt of
what is left
of summer light.

I lugged around the heavy book
bound in mossy forest
green, like the most devout child learning psalms:
Figures posed in mirth or tragedy
danced above the ballads, carols, hymns, sea-shanties,
marching songs, "Negro" spirituals.
Across the plain past roaming
antelope, I rode a bicycle built
for two, along the Erie canal, crossing
the Jordan by elephant in an endless procession
of pairs – to most, no one knew the tune, save
the ones that made me sad – a single bar
of "Down in the Valley" sunk me
in deepest grief, so I made the rest up, wedding the words
to melodies only mine, just me
and the bird and the son of a king,
onward the sea to Skye.

Nothing could have thrilled me more
than driving six white horses, fast,
around a bend, though I could not forget
the fate of the rooster, to say nothing of
Molly Malone; "Wayfaring
Stranger," "Careless Love," "Annie Laurie"
unbearably sad, though King Wenceslas
was clearly a very nice man and
the second verse to "Jingle Bells"
explained what without which,
one could never understand.

"Oh Susannah," "Scarborough Fair,"
 Joe Hill, alive as could be, Clementine,
whom none could save and I
drowned alongside each time; "Lord Lovel",
"Peter Gray"," "John Henry," "Barbara Allen":

Broken hearts
fallen like cherries, gathered and baked
into song – never was there a book
that held so much
of the world for which I longed.

A black and white photograph
creased at the belly
of a dark-haired nephew baby who choked
to death on a grape – family stories
condensed to epigrams
are most efficient for instilling
fear, and children must
have fear, they would say, lest
they become adults who thoughtlessly
pop peppermints into their mouths
without asking if those present
know Heimlich's maneuver.

A tiny shard of glass is found
in a church-sale square, a water glass
broken too near the batter
bowl – we are forbidden to eat
anything issuing from outside
a commercial kitchen, or ours
of course – children must have
fear, they would say, lest
they become adults who eat baked
goods indiscriminately and die
when sharp bits of negligence
make their way to the heart
(which they will).

The school is telephoned
in order to ascertain who is
the reckless one serving corn
for lunch, when it is a well-known fact
that unless chewed with great care,
corn, like an unripe apple, is as likely
as not to wind you up
in hospital – children must have
fear, they would say, lest
they become adults who eat
corn on the cob while talking and die
of otherwise perfectly preventable
indigestion.

Can one be stricken by lightning or only
struck – one day, I may find out, though
I have avoided both, thus far, be it
perhaps narrowly – it is true

a ball of fire
once travelled from the faucet
to the socket over the sink; true
my grandfather was thrown from the steps
onto the lawn on a merely overcast day – true
that the merit of lightning rods was
questionable, and that many odd things
happened there, and seemingly
nowhere else.

True, once the television was fried,
along with a range of small
appliances, and true the old maples
would likely have crushed us, had they fallen
onto the house, thus,
an altogether rational summertime fear:

"The electric-light-storm" would have us roused
from our beds, huddled in the dark back room
at first detection of a rumble,
my grandmother echoing each
thunder clap with a note so
high and pained, that the old dog, Mutt,
terror-stricken perhaps
at being struck, shook
like a mangy leaf, from the burrs
in his tail to his snout.

Now I lay me down to sleep,
I pray the Lord my soul
to keep; God bless: mommy, dad, grandpa,
grammy, mostly grandpa,
please let him not die
for a long time, very, and when
I get to heaven please
let there be
hypoallergenic horses – not ponies, real
horses that gallop and please
let them have saddles, both the English
and Western kind, and bridles and bits
and reins for sure but please, just this
one thing and it will be fine:
Please don't let
Grandpa die, not for a very
long time, at least until
I am grown up, please.

Please.   Amen.

By the green Sears table, not quite
   the colour of an avocado
(though we have not yet seen the inside of such a thing),
   by the window on the wall
in our house-trailer kitchen, a wedding
present to go with the Betty Crocker
cookbook, the cheeseball and ham
   canapés –
          twelve glass jars
sit on two narrow ledges, behind a lattice-
work gate – here is where
         our morning
ritual takes place:

My grandfather sits in the chair by the spice rack
and I on the table's edge, feet resting
on his knees, then
one by one, I reach
   for the oregano
       curry powder, sage
            nutmeg, cloves, allspice
                 coriander, cardamom, mace
  thyme and brick-
     red paprika, crushed pepper flakes –

cap unscrewed, I hold
   each to his nose –

                    he smells, takes a taste
as I watch his face, wait to hear
what he will say; each, so distinct, searching language
    to speak what makes it unique –
                is it a seed or a leaf or the bark of a tree –

and how was it found, brought all the way
                here, from we wonder where –
                                it is a bit
like this and a bit like that;
                he shakes his head in disbelief –

                        our spice-spell
never gets old –
                        we never lose
the twig-key
                    to the land of marvel
    and mystery

that belongs to
                    my grandfather and me,

    beyond our latticework

door of spices.

VERNAL

Eleven, my favorite
number, is stamped inside
the rubber, its good ga-losh
sound, stepping in and up and out
of shallow springtime
streams – you teach me
the difference between
rainbow and speckled; we cannot decide
which is prettier. Maroon
salamanders sun; I pick peppermint
so alive our eyes
water to chew a leaf, by the miniature
waterfalls, a song-line of pools,
springs coming down
the needle floor of pines.

We chase the stream
that snakes through the swale,
crossing cedar arteries red as old
blood in a throng of oval basins, I hear
the churning, softly the sound
your heart makes, always
wondering how many
beats remain.

Silver minnows swallow
the crumbs we toss them, glints
of sun unfurl
musky croziers in the clearing
that smells of bears;
Earth speaks vernal
truths to the fog and I am silent
as a deer so I might hear
if spring
will include you
in its promise.

We did not linger
in the machinery field, the time
we went alone, like we usually did
in the evening, so the men could admire
the latest innovations– impressive
to be sure, and alright for the farms
out west, but the combine did a damn poor job
of separating grain from straw from chaff –
it could not touch a threshing machine,
like the one that was yours and Grant's,
that you took to harvest barley and oats
way up to Baldwin's Mills.
And there never was a tractor half as good
as your '56 Massey-Harris 333, tomato-
red with yellow row-cropping wheels,
the archetype of a tractor, still
unmarred as the day you drove it home,
with its small silver key you let me turn,
and a more perfect sound there never
was nor will be
in the whole wide world.

We walked slow, your long limbs barely
bending at the knees, hanging back, letting me
lead by your littlest finger, as I did,
through the chicken barn until feathers
made us sneeze, admiring curious
breeds of lop-eared rabbit and quail;
guinea hens and hopeless ducks
honking for a pond; troubled turkeys
and a worried pair of peacocks,
then all the way to the other end
for the pretty Jersey calves, Guernseys,
Holsteins and the red and white
Ayrshires you admired; the Angus,
the Herefords, the pale
Charolais, like the old white bull
that pulled a sled and stopped
when you fell off, steering clear
of the horse barns that made me itch
and wheeze, but we saw the spotted
pigs and fed the goats and sheep.
I won a stuffed banana
when I pierced a balloon with a dart.

Then asking what I wished for next,
we looped back to the farmer's stall
(though the meat was nothing, compared to ours)
before we rested on the grandstand
for a bit, sipping cream soda or strawberry
Crush, as square-dancers twirled their frilly skirts,
do-si-do and allemande,
and when we walked out through
the Main Street gates and left the midway
noise behind, you asked if I was certain, sure
I'd seen enough, nodding to the neighbours
who were just coming in, and they
nodded back and winked at me
as I tried to match our steps.

A horse stepped on the neighbour's
daughter's head and for decades she screamed
in pain, so I could not have a horse
and that was that.

I longed until I could taste it and would not
be quelled; I carried on
about fetlocks, pintos and paints,
dappled grey, strawberry roan,
appaloosas, barrels, bridles, bits,
blazes and stars, as though
born of gypsies and slept every night
on leather and a chestnut
breast, roaming bareback
on a buckskin or a bay by day

and a pony
would not do – it had to be a horse, at least
fifteen hands, tall enough
to lift me into the sky, foreshadowing
a path checkered as a picnic
cloth, with all the makings of Eros
that later would turn to handsome
men.

Out of the blue, one day,
my grandfather says, I have his word:
He will see to it, knowing how much it means, that
I have a horse – words I never expected,
bursting me into tears,
though a curious
thing:

Having reached the point
of no return, my longing turned
cruelly inward, tampering
with biology in a strange twist
of fate – soon, getting within a quarter-
mile of said beast breaks me
into a burning, blistering welt
of hives;
coughing, sneezing, wheezing, watering,
swollen-shut eyes – my life
threatened
by merely a garment
worn by one who brushed a horse by –

a bell-clear message
that got straight to the point:

See –
        so now you know:

This.
        Is what love does.

IRON LUNG

You said
there were
even smaller ones
than those who stood on stools
behind the counter
at the midget-run store
off the highway – you saw them at night,
at the freak show, at the fair
when you were a kid – there was even
a swaddled midget baby in its midget
mother's arms; once, two
brothers, the first albino, the second black;
a pair of Siamese twins
with double sets of teeth, but the girl
is what kept you
from sleep –
you were haunted
by the ceaseless rasping, never
erased from your mind, the death-
sound of bellows; the prettiest
songbird trapped
in a tomb of lead – to imagine
a blue-eyed butterfly's
wings weighted
with heaviest chains, sweet
sixteen in an iron
lung, behind a freak-show
wall of glass.

A stained silk purse once
dyed lavender to match the dress

for a cousin's reception, a generation
or two gone by, is where I put the letters
you found in the lath of the wall. I am
a keeper of things forgotten, a vase

for pictures made by words, a riverbed
for the stories you tell, an earthen silhouette

of a child – I know the ghosts of the children
who lived and died here – grass grows
between the wheels; I stuff dry
leaves into beaded satchels dangling
from the peddlers' wagons, I bang
the tin and silver pans; I am sad
for the dancing bear; I am awed

by the elephant on its way to the next show
stalled on the Way's Mills bridge; I hear
the whistle of the steam engine, gape
at wingless bodies of steel bound for the war, I walk

in the forgotten forest graveyard, where a yellow
rosebush grows, I nod to the father

of twelve who walks back home
through a snow-covered field at dawn, all night
cutting firewood by the light of a lantern.

I hear the old man you carried
down from his bed before fire collapsed
the beams, crying for his suit on the hook behind
the door –
now what would he wear to his funeral?

A foot of black mud where the frogs
spent winters, lived at the bottom
finer than silk and grey
clay, beneath the cattails where red-winged
blackbirds perched as sentinels, guarding nests
no one ever saw, flashing their
scarlet symmetry, gliding from fencepost to fencepost
like generals surveying from the top
of each ridge,
through the loom
of giant dancers, the willow's wicker cages
sashaying to wind's serenade to sky; the accordion
bellows of frog-legs – spotted turquoise
leopards; the flighted avatars – dragon-
flies; water-skimming pond-skaters
defying natural law – I want to make a raft,
drift just like Huck
through the starry marsh
marigolds at midnight, my little sister,
a loaf of bread and a string for catching
minnows; under the moon
with a long birch stick, lying in wait
for surprise, endless as summer
through the moats of cloud castles.

Our white river
in the woods
was bright as strands
of pearl, lit from within as if
the sun-lit moon had broken off
a gift; we would wade in
to search for pure
specks of gold, perfect
crystal into which we would look
long and hard, trying to fathom
its wisdom.

It had been one
quartz monolith,
and it had taken quite a few sticks
to blast it, a damn shame
you said, to destroy such
a beautiful thing,–
you might have hit
the jackpot, a vein of
solid gold but instead
it was hauled away, truckload
after truckload,
for paths to the pavilions
of Man and His World.

*"A geological wonder in Stanstead East
on its way to the world's fair "*
read the '67 clipping
kept in the clock,
and still enough remained
to flow a long white river,
a stone mirror for the moon
who may find her
reflection there still, in the woods
where the witch hazel hangs
with the damp lace of bone-
pale spiders.

It was not just
us – there *was*
something
magnetic, compelling, even
binding – anyone stopped
for water because
their car was overheating,
or to use the telephone
(*how easy to remember:*
four 4s, they always said); friends
and acquaintances, friends
of friends of friends, always
found a reason to
return, as if there
was something
they had left or forgotten;
as if something
had gotten in
their blood,
drawing them
back to the source, and
at a loss, they were,
to understand
just what
that something
was.

The closet
was too large
to be a closet and too small
to be a room, though for a time, as a kid,
my mother had a bed there,
off the room where a pencil
with the Queen on it, from the visit of '39,
rested on the frame of the door.

Behind the nesting
Samsonite, yellowed curtains and chenille, a leather
case of old receipts and deeds;
a dark passage
led to a series of doors
unto chambers,
where forms within forms
held prisms guarding secrets
terrifying to behold, but further
in, late one night
I found something
rare; strange – I covered it
with lamp black
and in the corner
it stayed –

when I knew
that it was lost to me,
or had been
given away, in earnest
I began my search
for what it was and
what remained.

The schoolhouse was
just up the road
and a stage-coach stop
at old man Marion's; at one time
there was a church – they said it
burned to the ground, but I swear
you could hear an echo
of an echo of its bell in the clay
bricks strewn amidst
the gravel
in our dooryard.

A stone-lined hell-deep well in our cellar,
meant that once, a man
had been all the way down there – our water
having long been piped from springs
across the road, the well's purpose
was a mystery to the oldest
memory – one hardly dares to tell
what had happened
down there
one winter's night: a travelling husband,
two daughters, a mother gone
insane, and an axe –
in my own mother's time,
still were the stains
along the beams by the stairs – one
possible explanation for the upstairs bed
unmade, after it was, and things
like haircombs or a necklace
ending up
other than where it was left, or why

ghost stories
told in that house, being neither
fiction nor benign, frightened
the ones who told them
even more than those
who listened, wishing
they'd declined.

Three great-aunts, Helen, Lily,
and Maggie, come to visit on Sundays
with the great-uncles, a pause
from their town-lives. Maggie is a half
great-aunt, sharing only a mother
with my grandfather, her father having
died young of a rare cancer, less than a year
after they arrived, leaving Maggie's mother,
Susan, alone with baby Maggie in the cold
of a Quebec winter, so much colder, back then.
What choice did she have but to say yes
to the man who brought her food
and firewood? How could she have known?
Such an accent she must have had, her words
still alive with old sounds.

Maggie is short with hourglass
proportions, red hair, freckles, flashing hazelnut
eyes, looks from her father, as Helen and Lily
are tall, with the same odd posture, stooping
shoulders, gangly limbs, blue eyes. They wear full
skirts with gathered-in waists to hide
pouched-out bellies, the only place anything
sticks out, their light hair curled into the style
of the day; they are the same, but different, voices
dissimilar and their houses each have a particular
smell. The great-uncles have town-jobs
in by-the-hour shops and buy new appliances
and dining sets on credit, to sit at when they walk
home for lunch.

In spite of many ardent courters, Maggie
never marries, having reasons not to trust
a man; her apartments are cluttered with *Enquirers*,
hard-bound romance novels, jewellery boxes,
hand-knit muffs, odd bits from church bazaars, anything
with a thistle or a bit of tartan, things
destined as gifts to us.

They visit to spread and gather gossip,
show off a new car, recount the details
of a recent operation, play a few
rounds of cards, and the sisters visit
to come back home, out to the farm, they call it,
and when they leave, they tell us
we really must come to see
them, and we follow them out to their cars
and wave, wishing them a careful drive.

My grandfather's father Ernest's gang
had been around a while already, when
Ernest heard of Susan Patterson, Scotswoman
with the baby out on Boynton,
husband had just died – a spell with brothers
Gene and Ralph earning big tips as bellhops
in New York and Boston's grand hotels,
Ernest had just bought himself a farm
an hour's walk from where he grew up,
a white clapboard house with dark green trim,
half a dozen sheds and barns; twenty-six cleared acres
on one side, three-hundred or so
wooded across the road. Gene went as far
west as a man could, bought a farm
that met the Pacific – one day Ralph
got off a train and came walking across
the Oregon field where Gene was hilling potatoes –

"By God, if it isn't Ralph, how the hell are ya?"
What happened after that, I never heard.

There is an extremely small possibility
that Ernest was not born
a villain, that wielding a butcher's
knife to wake his family well before dawn
was merely a symptom of a chemical
imbalance –
whatever it was, it poured down on
generations, causing bar fights that blinded
men, rage that billowed like storm clouds
all the way across fields to neighbouring
towns; a terror of death should he be
waiting, a namesake for men
who shared genes with the famous pilgrim
who glorified nights spent scalping Indians –
something in the ground,
Susan from the lowlands had said, over
and over, she said that
something was wrong here, poor Susan, who left
a hard life for a harder one, and brought
every old-world ghost with her.

SUSAN

I only know about the overcoat
her father wore at night to hide
the fish he speared from the Firth
of Forth; that he was a Lowlands crofter.

I only know that in spring, the year
before the *Titanic* sailed, she bade
farewell to all that she knew.

I only know she was back in the field, hoeing
potatoes, the day after her children
were born, and sometimes out there, she sang
in the old language.

I only know my great-grandmother made
bread every single day, and once
with raisins that sunk to the bottom.

I only know that somewhere a rocking chair
is considered hers; that my mother
remembers her casket in the unheated
front room.

I only know that every woman after her
believed that she could hear them, and in
silence spoke her name

when darkness ascended as if
from a split in the earth's core; when tempers
raged like molten rock and dread
sat high in the stomach

and if I knew
more than that, I might not
say, for fear of raising yet more
troubled ghosts with my words.

She grew up Anglican, talking to saints,
and it was true
the smell of roses broke out at times:
"That means my prayer will be answered," she would say.
Lovely, was her handwriting in letters that pled;
a schoolteacher she wanted to be, but went to wash
bedclothes, the summer after fifth grade.
At the big lake rooming-house, water
snakes scared her and later fifty-six
hours a week at the glove shop, all the pay
to her mama, Emma, a large, gruff woman come up
from the South, giving five pretty daughters coal-black
hair, powder-fine skin, and never a flinch of shyness –
     come hell
or high water, my grandmother could procure anything
she saw our heart was set on, aright any
injustice – she'd pick up that black
receiver and pretend to be
anyone – call the plow-man, the weather-man,
the principal to close the school before snow
ever started; call Sears, call the mayor, call
the butcher, of course, everyone
in the town knew Mildred and the phone book
was thick in those days – more selfless she was
than anyone – ironed irreversible creases

in my good black jeans and called them
slacks – her advice, I ignored, from how
laundry absolutely must be hung, ways
to use Bisquick, how to beat the devil
in Solitaire, to the evils of ending up
with a lazy man, warning what would befall
all of us, should I fail to understand.

I see her now running
a comb through her hair in the rearview
mirror, still thick and black after
the chemo – she told me as we sped to town
that driving was easy, not much to it
but steering – it was a miracle, everyone
said, that she never took the ditch; that
she never had pain, even when it reached
her bones; how everyone
in her room that day
smelled roses.

The Round Oak
stood by the door to the front room,
a stout mother who never left
the kitchen in a hundred years,
in a long black cast-iron apron, her wide
underbelly's bolted cracks
from water thrown on flames
one night before the rest headed out
to a dance.

Infinite sparks, the iron
poker kindled, echo upon echo
in its dark chamber stirring
coals, a motion so repetitive, after
so many years, perhaps

it held
the sound – you would hear it
in the evening, all the way
from the back kitchen,
where we sat in the summer-
thrum of crickets, behind the closed door
where she stood alone
with lilacs in a milk-
glass vase perched on her top like a hat –
you would hear

the latch
slowly
lifting, the high rasping
notes of
the hinge; the poker's
reaming clangs
from the inside, then
the iron-on-iron
of a satisfied jaw.

DISHES

The women stood with their hands
in the water, their backs to the voices, other
messes – sometimes
glancing at what lay out the window, or for some
not a window, but a mirror they could check in
for improved or worsened lines – sometimes
for after, there was an Avon hand cream
dispenser, in the shape of a bird
or an ear of corn.

The women stood with their hands
 in the water, in all kinds of weather
(except lightning) – sometimes they hurried
to be finished for the next task or
just to sit down – most often they were unaware
of the dishes, beyond the deeming of dirty
or clean, and sometimes they stood there,
with slowed deliberation, so feelings
could arrange into acceptable
phrases before turning to face
the room. Sometimes

things broke down
there, and cut them in the murky
water; sometimes it would not go down
even by the will of the plunger – sometimes
their rings slipped off from the soap,
and their hands were strange
and nervous, but a thing
they never, ever did, regardless
of their age or the hour, was to get
into bed before their sink was
empty, dried, and polished.

OTHER GRANDMOTHER

To whom I was one of many; she, the favourite
of none; whom we visited out of obligation, in a place

called Tomifobia, calling hell-ohh-oh and after a long
wait, out she comes, pinching

cheeks, exclaiming: "Oh mercy me, oh
my," frazzled by an unexpected visitor

amidst days talking to chickadees
and squirrels; old smells fill the doorway, mothballs,

leaking pipes, vinyl tablecloths infused with decades
of woodsmoke; a half-apron tied

across her odd little belly, she rushes
to seat us in turned-wood chairs reserved

for such events, showing us her latest greeting cards
lined up on the sideboard, sent by relatives

who care no more, no less, than the cost of
a stamp; in summer she walks us around her old world

roses, her pansies, the chosen stones, carefully
placed to edge her little lawn, under

the arching willows that sing to her;
they are chopped away, as soon as she is gone.

In a blasted rock hole through the burning
days of summer, salt pills to keep him
from waning; through the bitterest winds of winter
that got trapped down there, he drilled in that
deafening din – I think
there were a few good years; a young picture
shows him smiling, before the channel bar, the fog
of dust and the derrick, named for an Elizabethan
executioner.

The sad part was home
was no sinecure. I remember his grey lunch
box by the sink, his head asleep on the table
before supper, his anger at any kind
of noise, but when the old friends came down
in August, his voice took on a lyrical
layer, and they talked all night
about the engines, the antics,
the good old days – he did love
the cars, the music he heard in bars, perhaps
the idea of a woman
who would set things right –
my mother must have tried, but hers was
a world that could hold no
one's dreams – some mistakes
are tenacious, keeping you down so long
bones set in postures – then on a Tuesday
morning in November, he was standing at his drill
in the rain; his back to the giant rolling
runaway tire, and the boys watched in horror
his gallows and could not warn him,
through the dust and the deafening
din, as the tire headed straight
for him, and the next day
his casket was closed.

Ole Fred, one of a throng
of haphazard visitors to pull
into the yard out of the blue
to pay respects and offered a lowball
from a forty ounce of Gordon's.

Ole Fred with the guitar he
was born playing and never left
home without, with a beer in one
hand and a smoke stuck
in the first fret.

Ole Fred who never hurt a fly,
no less a flea, with a voice like gravel
under a rusty Buick rolling
nice and slow.

Ole Fred who had a garage beside his house
on a back road to nowhere and worked cheap
for any poor bastard needing a patch-job
or a weld to hold "at least for now."

One might ask, why write
a poem about Fred – my answer is
because

no one else
in this world is ever going to.

The gin never helped
much that I could see – at the kitchen table
they sat and no one left (the usual loyal suspects)
   until the bottle was out
or several;
  sooner or later, one or the other,
hand on the shoulder of the fellow
   to his left or his right: *This here ... this here*
... is one hell of
a man ... now who would I be ... Christ only knows ...
 one hell
of a man ... is a damn good friend ... best damn
friend a man ever had ... since we're talking shit, what
 else do we
have, anyway, when you think
about it a minute ... all I'm trying to say, now you
listen to me good ... cuz I never said this to ya
before ... is
you been a damn good
friend ... an I'll tell ya right to yer face, sure
as I am living, if I make it
through the night ... you're one
hell
of
a man ... hell of a friend, did I ever tell ya, and so it went
on, my grandfather nodding *well, now wait*
just a minute

ya bastard ... I could say the same to you,
one foot in his chair,
a bent knee reaching his nose, a lit Winston
in his left and a glass in his right

and the women
           summoned to sit on the men's knees tried
   their best to smile
as they held their breath against
   the juniper and the ferment
and silently pled
   for calm
to reign,
tonight.

SOUNDTRACK

For all the damage done by pride,
it was nothing to laugh at, how easy it was
to love Loretta; listen to "Okie from
Muskogee" just the way Merle
meant it – they were cynical about the man,
but not about the mettle it took
to forget just enough
of yesterday to get up out of bed;
songs that drank to the sadness
at the marrow: the steel
guitar affirmed
we would not be beaten, whether cheated by
Jolene, or left
by Lucille – the music forewarned
no one got out alive – we were all in it
together, if we made it through
December, all of us were bound
for the burning
ring of fire, though we
never needed reminding –
we knew life was good, so long
as the ground under our feet
was ours: the green, green
grass of home was all
we had, and all that mattered.

EGLANTINE

Vetch and bladder
campion by the mailbox,
blue flag, cattail, cowslips
in the pond;

strawberry, ground ivy, four-
leaved clovers any time my grandmother
looked down; bluebells under the picture

window, dark rose peony crawling
with ants; burdock in the maples
by the roadside; wild columbine
along the ditch;

lily of the valley behind the kitchen in the sumac
grown into fern; white, lavender, magenta
lilacs off the veranda's far end;

Indian paintbrush, sorrel, yarrow, buttercup,
timothy in the unmown field; hollyhock
along the wharfing, chokecherry to the west;

the wild rose or eglantine
east of the apple by the corner of the barn.

THE MAPLES

The maples were old, even when my grandfather
was a kid, meeting in an arch over the road
as if to frame the picture of a memory.

You could lose yourself in the canopies,
on your back in the grass, trace time in the grey
furrows of their bark; you could hold what you could
not tell anyone, in the massive, gracious angles of
their limbs.

You could drink the water they gave you
at winter's end, on its way up from the earth, and
they were none the weaker for having given it, for there
was always gallons and gallons more.

You could toss their samaras high in the air,
and the way they would come down, would make you
consider things in pairs, like the house
you were born in, amidst all those you are not.

You could rake their leaves to bank the stone
of the house, so it would hold the fires of winter,
when you could see each wound, scar, lost limb,
and know where they grew beyond, and where
they stayed the same.

When the moon threw shadows between
their branches, a labyrinth of light was cast,
and if you followed it in, you could not tell
a dream from the future or past.

When one was deemed dangerous and could no longer
stand, we held watch, stiff as soldiers, unable to utter
a sound, mourning not only the tree but all
it had seen, since even before my grandfather
was a kid.

Before or after you sold the cows
was time's reference – you were sick
for days, when they loaded them;
evening and no sound of bells
drawing near, the old collie sent off
to fetch them, udders heaving
as they waltzed from the top pasture
down the lane, slow hooves
on cement, taking their same
places in the stanchions, waiting
for the milker, as you spoke
to them low and soft, but

things were changing, and had been
for a while, since the advent of quota,
going up and up; more regulation
all the time – used to be
you'd take the cream to town, the skim
fed to the calves, but you went along and built
the milk house for the agitator-paddled tank,
the price of milk now depending
on the content of cream of the herd –
many were calling it a day: "Get big or get out",
having reached all the way to us, so
I barely remember
when the water troughs flowed clean;
the white-washed stalls, or how it was
on a winter's night – the warmth, the creak
of the hinge; the old wooden door swinging
back to a sky lit with stars, like it was

on Christmas Eve
when my mother was a kid, the peaceful
patient sound of chewing cud,
like something that always
will be and always
was; the sweet smell
of hay, ambling through the aisles, knowing
that when

the clock struck midnight and all
were asleep, the animals
would speak as men.

In dreams, another world began
beyond the wet corner of the field, a river
charting a path for me to follow, shallow
in places and I entered; in others deep
and damned, strung with grey wooden
bridges that threatened to give way
and there
in a narrow, fast-flowing stream, once I
let go, as though holding had lost
its purpose and I dared to
move on, loosing
my grip on the rock to which
I clung against the downstream
force, losing fear for a split
of a second, body unburdened,
drifting, the opposite
of all I had known: I entered that
source of the flooding, waves deep
as an ocean over the field – I never
learned to swim, though here
I did not sink, but was held
aloft, swept all the way
out under the stars,
back to the doorstep
again and again.

SACRIFICE

You were
a perfect compass,
your long arm rising, pointing north, a game
we played in windowless hospital
rooms, a knowing born of years
through forests and fields, from dawn to dusk
tracking wild things on foot
until you could not lose your way, like
Thoreau, walking twenty miles
or more in a day.

After days of watching the blood
pool ever darker, when we know it is hopeless and
your leg is sawn off like wood; when delirium and
morphine wane, the primitive urge to walk
the earth again as a man, roars up to cleave
your heart and in a moment of desperate
hopefulness, you are gleeful as a child,
describing in detail how you will fashion
one of smoothest ash.

Through the hall window,
I am there to watch the car pull in
the yard to bring you home, from car to chair
as they wheel you up
the newly built ramp –
through the curtains,
I do not dare
to look
at your eyes – I see the way your mouth
is closed tight against this travesty
of nature, this curse
of heredity, this
               sacrifice
of man.

"Do you think she'll be there?"
he asked her on his deathbed, and she
answered: *"Yes, dear, I am sure she will."*

More than thirty years since
she had died in her sleep, the wife
of a crippled cousin, the woman with whom he'd
run around – her picture
in his wallet until
his last belongings were placed
in the bag with his name.

Green eyes, freckles, and, unlike
my grandmother, willow-waisted and god
knows what
would have happened, had she not had
a heart defect, or swallowed
a bottle of pills.

We had good times
and we had bad times, but
the good outweighed the bad,
my grandmother said – I don't know
if she believed
those words as they left her lips,
though I do know she meant it
when she said:
"Yes dear, she will be there. I am sure she will."

LORD OF THE ELEMENTS

There is little
a forest will not forgive –
that is why you went, I think

and stayed for hours and
hours, just sitting,
lying on the ground, observing patterns
of the seasons, things absolved of
fate, the creatures who knew
their place in the chain
of beasts
and never longed to understand
things gone wrong;

a wild green protection
enveloping, a kindness
despite; reasons sunken
deep into moss and the rest
distilled to dew

that you drank in
quiet communion,
in a rapture lit
by the setting sun,
among the ones
you belonged with,
before the lord
of the elements.

GARDEN

A flat stone found to sharpen
the axe, then east
in the afternoon we are off to cut rails
for the Lincoln peas

– always a pair, two
to a hill, for beans, wax and green; lengthwise,
the handle of the hoe makes a row
when distant birches leaf;

when apple blossoms have gone
with the wind, we lay the husks
of seed into long, shallow graves to rest
beneath the velvet loam;

the sunflowers to the north will rise,
looking down on the black cat
bathing in the dirt and me
weaving twine and tendrils.

Earth sifts sand through our hands
in my first and your last
garden; the tilled dirt, our hourglass
as lettuce rises to a milky
point, faster than we think;
we eat each bitter
leaf with toast and onion
greens, to the song of evening frogs
in the kitchen that has seen it all before.

Swiss chard roils – we fish it out
of salted boiling water; the mineral
taste on the back of our throats
is more truth that we can bear,
sunlit days go by, fierce red
radishes bob in their bowl of ice;

the black cat rolls, raising dust
between the nip and the dill; parsley
worms turn into swallowtail
butterflies, our single summer
savory becomes a blood
red burning bush.

After a long night of hail and a hard
early frost; a wind from the north, and
it is only me; next, the black cat
wavers a second too long
under an evening snow-plow's wheel

but the ground still holds
the fossil, fallen from its cord, that I
wore tied-loose around my neck

that spring, before the world
changed,

when we walled the angels
into a square

and called it

       our Garden.

We sit in the dark on the edge
of the bed and you start in the middle

of stories you never wanted
to tell, your voice a different
timbre, strange
and looming as what we await. I wheel your chair
to the bathroom, make us another cup of tea.

After long weeks, months, when I
look into the mirror, I see you
looking back; when my fingertips
brush my forearm, I am your arm
touching me; my hand
on your arm is my arm under
your hand – I cannot stop thinking

how the first time we saw the ocean,
we drove to the end of the road and there
was the sea – your eyes a watery sky
blue – just exactly,
you said, like you always thought it would be.

You rose before dawn,
while we were asleep, so it would be
just you and the tide – if
you could draw a line straight across, you said …
telling me where we would be.

How you revelled in that ceaselessness
of waves returning to shore, every day
since forever, again and again you said
in slightly different ways.

Again and again, I rise from the floor
where I've made a bed
beside yours, rising with you
when the thought of being lost
to infinity makes you panic – in the dark
behind you, my arms
wrapped around yours, we ride on the waves
of fear, then you start in the middle
of stories you never wanted
to tell, as though you cannot go
before the last has washed to shore.

I wheel your chair to the bathroom,
make us another cup of tea; in the mirror
above the sink again: there is you, and not me.

Moonlight through the window, from the edge
of the bed, we look out into the dark
tide, your eyes ever bluer,
the closer it comes to shore – I am walking
with you into the waves
further than we thought I could, with you, into
that ceaselessness, as far
as love.

Yarrow tea
infused in jars by night,
concoctions from the old
books that I hoped
would give us longer.
In the stillness of time having
lifted, our vision chiseled as
colour and form bled into
nature's order, in the way
only death allows.

An old woman came,
in those last days, in the sumac outside
the bedroom window – she stirred
deep copper baths of dye
in shades of burnished
fall; she gathered fern, was dressed
in fern, had uncut silver
hair – familiar she was,
although I did not
know from where
I knew her – her colours
stayed, though her form
left before I could ask her.

If you ask a man, say a farmer
with a week or less to live, if there is
anything he still wants
to say, he might tell you about the day

his father died, in January of the year
the war ended, how he traced his little sister's
name in the thick frost of the barn window,
and told her, no, Lily, not ever, when she asked
if he was coming back.

He may tell you that if he had it to do over,
he would grow a market garden, no
animals this time, how it just about
killed him every time a cow he raised from calf
was loaded on the truck for slaughter.

He may tell you about the woman
he loved though both were married, how
black her hair, how red her lips
were, the way she kissed him right on
the mouth and how he does not remember
even once, his mother having held him.

He may tell you he would have liked
to see the West, live in Alaska
for a time all by himself, on no more
than he could track, hunt, or forage.

He may tell you, saying he knows
it sounds a little crazy, but that he thinks
he could have been a picture-painter; how once
as a kid, he found something
with strings like a guitar – no one knew,
but in secret he learned how to play it, and
it sounded pretty good.

He may tell you he never prayed
or thought much of church, but
alone in the woods, in the quiet, a strange
kind of peace came, that seemed like
it must be God.

And it is not so much the words
that you will remember, but
the way that they are said, the worlds
his eyes still hold, as he says them.

DOORBELL

That year someone had cut down
the hydrangeas, as never should be done, and no
cream-coloured flowers flanked either side of
the steps, where we sat and watched the end
of summer play its games, by

the round white rock flecked with mica
under the green front-door
bell that rang a perfect ding-dong – things
inside you were failing – they took you away

and brought you back again and again
that year – you changed, I saw each change
remove you, yet when you saw me in the garden
through the summer kitchen window

in my new rummage-sale straw hat, you said:
Next year, let's put five rows of the green beans

next to the peas – absence, the taking
away, is a language
that cannot be learned – the house

that held you from the beginning, knew no more
what to do with itself than I did, when
it heard – the eastern sun was still
the same for a time, coming up over the woods
but for days, the wind took anything untethered
for a joyride through the yard.

Faithful to the seasons is that echo, coming up like water
from the ground – a gust in the night that will not settle,
caught in the chambers of a flue – I think

about that round white rock flecked with mica,
    so long gone
now, no one remembers it but me and how the perfect
ding-dong of the green front-doorbell
is whorled in a two-note helix with some filament
of my brain, but gone

as though it never was, is the way
you said my name.

REQUIEM

We saw the end
coming through shadows
in the willows along the broken
brook, as if you knew
all would be
lost, once you were gone.

Hedgerows, the copse
sheared to the ground, waste
laid to the woods-road
from the skidder, springs
muddied, even the eyes
of the house – the doors,
windows replaced and burned;

bears hunted, sheds torn down,
the trees we planted
felled – as if you knew all
that would die with you, you took
a long time leaving,
ebbing, flowing
through nights and weeks and days,
until we knew
that *we* had to let open
the door to let you through.

The clocks stopped,
as Auden said, and visions
of a desert crept in: I knew
that nothing, now could
come to any good – the end
was at hand and looking back, I see
as if through a storm of sand –

perhaps, as in the old forgotten tale,
one day the willows again
will speak, telling all
that I left out –

a reed sprung from a pool of a slain
daughter's blood, became a pipe that sang
her ballad – if such a withy
springs from our stream in a hundred years,
a wind from the west may sing up our saga,
as only song could.

THE HAWK

We walked that day, my mother and I,
up the woods-road past the springs,
the cedars, the turtlehead, the brambles
growing through the hoods of cars
come and gone.

Through the new field you made
with your brother, Grant; the alfalfa –
we walked the road we had taken only
with you – we had never gone alone

though we were
not alone – you were there
that day before the funeral:
in the trees, in the wind; the changing
leaves of old October – you were not
separate from sky nor space
between the calls of birds.

A hawk
had flown above us all the way,
the morning we left
the hospital – in life, you hated hawks
for killing the innocent
swallows – though this bird
would not leave us,
leading the hearse all the way from town
to the graveyard west of the barn, circling
our procession, waiting in the sky

when the long black car
stopped to fix a flat on Fairfax;
pausing as the convoy gasped
at the woodland crown turned as if
by lathe, of the noble buck
that leapt across our road.

The way it was
in the woods that autumn day
did not last, as nothing can, and
by the time the sun had set over the new-dug grave,
the hawk was nowhere to be seen and you were
faraway.

CABIN

What happened to the pretty screen door,
the cabin you built in the woods

when you were forty-four, the fence,
the gate, the cot on the screened veranda,

where you would sleep to hear the night
cries of bobcats – what happened

to the tiny pot-bellied stove with its pan,
the card table with its deck of cards, the picture

book of mountain lions; what happened to the sun-
splotched photograph taken when light

could still enter that part of the woods, of you
in a maroon shirt with rolled-up sleeves,

me, not yet a thought, and my mother, a kid
in bell-bottoms –

At the field's edge, the house;
barn and sheds behind; twelve
panes each of window glass,
shutters long lost.

Clapboard the colour of goldenrod
before gone to seed; hollyhocks
against barnboard to the south;

floorboards sawn from the pines,
northeast the swamp of cedars; latch-door
to the cellar between the doors
to the hall and the room
you were born in.

Cellar cupboard holds pickles
no one dares to eat; trap door leads to
nothing.

Shed-chamber stairs and old iron
once a part of something,
you have to walk on to get to
the spider the size of a saucer, wrapping up
another horsefly

Door of the front bedroom closet
won't stay shut through the night,
not even with the nail you have driven in
and bent back and around; sound
of the poker reaming the ashes
but no one is in
the kitchen.

By the hedge
at the end of the dooryard,
where you fed corn to crows,
the Massey-Harris shines
like an apple on a stick at the fair;
the drawbar, the clevis-pin, and the wagon
with the moth-chewed pillow from
the chesterfield.

Late afternoon sun
between boards of the haymow;
no calves in the pen.

Hay-rake rusts by the blackberry bush;
water troughs won't fill; tin on the milk-house
roof creaks; weathervane says wind blows
northeast.

Across the road by the pond, damselflies hover
like airborne sapphire matchsticks; cowslips
bloom in tufts of grass
in the brook where hooves have been;

to the west, hedgerow trees,
filigree to the sun that sets; nowhere
is the sky so high –

I had the dream again last night –
I dreamed I'd said the word

You had called,
and I had answered:

I was coming back home to you.

From
the red wagon,
I tried to record
everything

we passed – words
flew through my head –
the world
went by too fast

but if
the blackbird
told me one
thing, it is that when

like the ebony
jewelwing's
sheath, I fall
to ash,

from the old spring,
again
we will drink
in the light
of the sun,
where grows
wintergreen.

"EBONY JEWELWING"

The ebony jewelwing (*Calopteryx maculata*) is a species of damselfly found near streams in the Eastern United States and Southeastern Canada, ranging west to the Great Plains. The male has a metallic blue-green body and black wings.

"WEDDING PICTURES"

In the field of auto mechanics, the term "throw a rod" means that a "connecting rod" (the metal part that connects the piston to the crankshaft) has broken off. When this happens, one of two things occurs: If the rod breaks while the piston is on its way up, the piston keeps going up until it lodges permanently into the cylinder head. If the rod breaks while the piston is coming down, the broken rod can pierce a hole through the engine block. The engine is instantly ruined in either event.

"BEFORE AND AFTER THE COWS"

In the 1970s, encouraging the growth of corporate factory farms, President Nixon's secretary of agriculture, Earl Butz, urged farmers to "*get big or get out,*" causing millions of farmers to take on debt in order to conform to new policies that penalized small-scale producers. In the 1980s, when interest rates spiked and farm incomes plunged, tens of thousands of farms across North America were forced to foreclose.

ACKNOWLEDGMENTS

Putting this collection together was an exercise in
gratitude, and I would be remiss not to formally thank
all those who made it what it is: Willow Grant Moller,
for his unrelenting sense of humour amidst long days of
editing; Joel B. Levine, my dearest ally and the greatest
writer I know, for the crystalline insights and enthusiasm
of his matchless mind; Marjorie Bruhmuller, poet and
earthly angel, for her tireless attention through
innumerable "latest versions"; Alexandre Bergeron; the
long thread of individuals who one way or another laid
the stepping-stones: Gabriel Safdie, Shelley Pomerance,
Mark Abley, Angela Leuck, Allan Hepburn, David
Drummond, and all the kind people at MQUP; those
who read early versions of my manuscript and encouraged
me with kind reviews; my coracle of fellow biography-
workers who raised me to the task; and last but foremost,
those who from the other side made their whispers
audible – to them, and to the spirits of place, my gratitude
knows no bounds.

PREVIOUSLY PUBLISHED WORKS

- "The Fair," *Small Farmer's Journal* (Fall 2022), edited by Lynn R. Miller
- "Ebony Jewelwing," LEAP: *The Leslie Strutt Memorial Chapbook, LCP* (December 2021+)
- "Ebony Jewelwing," *New Millennium Writings Anthology* (2022, online and in print)
- "The House," FONT *Magazine* (December 2021), edited by Rachel McCrum
- "Weathervane," "Dishes," "Afternoons," "Doorbell," "Mildred," Anthology: *Emergence: Contemporary Women Poets of Quebec's Eastern Townships* (Studio Georgeville, 2021), edited by Angela Leuck
- "Weathervane," *Taproot IV* (Lennoxville: Townshippers' Association, 2009)